W9-BMN-055

Reading STREET

Program Authors

Peter Afflerbach

Camille Blachowicz

Candy Dawson Boyd

Wendy Cheyney

Connie Juel

Edward Kame'enui

Donald Leu

Jeanne Paratore

P. David Pearson

Sam Sebesta

Deborah Simmons

Sharon Vaughn

Susan Watts-Taffe

Karen Kring Wixson

PEARSON

Scott Foresman

Editorial Offices: Glenview, Illinois • Parsippany, New Jersey • New York, New York
Sales Offices: Boston, Massachusetts • Duluth, Georgia • Glenview, Illinois
Coppell, Texas • Sacramento, California • Mesa, Arizona

We dedicate Reading Street to
Peter Jovanovich.

His wisdom, courage,
and passion for education
are an inspiration to us all.

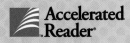

About the Cover Artist

Daniel Moreton lives in New York City, where he uses his computer to create illustrations for books. When he is not working, Daniel enjoys cooking, watching movies, and traveling. On a trip to Mexico, Daniel was inspired by all of the bright colors around him. He likes to use those colors in his art.

ISBN-13: 978-0-328-24343-3
ISBN-10:   0-328-24343-4

Copyright © 2008 Pearson Education, Inc.

All Rights Reserved. Printed in the United States of America. This publication is protected by Copyright, and permission should be obtained from the publisher prior to any prohibited reproduction, storage in a retrieval system, or transmission in any form by any means, electronic, mechanical, photocopying, recording, or likewise. For information regarding permission(s), write to: Permissions Department, Scott Foresman, 1900 East Lake Avenue, Glenview, Illinois 60025.

5 6 7 8 9 10 V063 16 15 14 13 12 11 10 09 08
CC:N1

Dear Reader,

A new school year is beginning. Are you ready? You are about to take a trip along a famous street—*Scott Foresman Reading Street.* On this trip you will meet exciting characters, such as a pig in a wig, a blue ox, and a dinosaur.

As you read the stories and articles, you will gain exciting new information that will help you in science and social studies.

While you're enjoying these exciting pieces of literature, you will find that something else is going on—you are becoming a better reader, gaining new skills and polishing old ones.

Have a great trip, and send us a postcard!

Sincerely,
The Authors

Read It
Online
PearsonSuccessNet.com

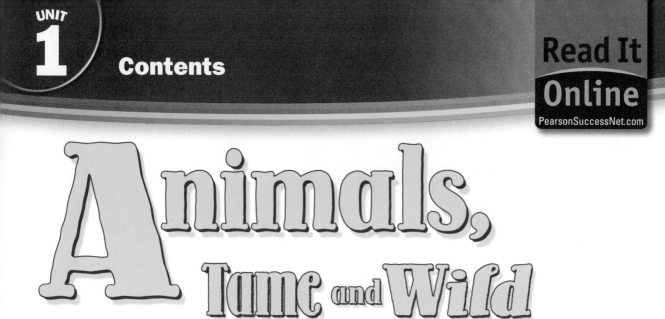

Animals, Tame and Wild

How are people and animals important to one another?

Animal Friends

Wild Animals

Read It
Online
PearsonSuccessNet.com

Animals, Tame and Wild

How are people and animals important to one another?

9

Let's Talk About
Animal Friends

Words to Read

on

way

in

Read the Words

1. Sam the cat is on my lap.

2. He ran that way.

3. Sam ran in the sack.

Sam, Come Back!

Genre: Fiction

Fiction stories are made-up stories. Next you will read about Sam and Jack, who are made-up characters.

Sam, Come Back!

by Susan Stevens Crummel

illustrated by Janet Stevens

Who is Sam, and where did he go?

Sam the cat is on my lap.

Sam ran. Sam, come back!

Sam ran that way.
Nab that cat!

See Sam in the sack.

Sam ran that way.
Nab that cat!

See Sam in the pack.

Bad Sam! Sam, come back!

Jack, Jack! Sam is back.
Pat Sam on my lap.

Think and Share

Talk About It Did the author write a funny story? Find and read one part of the story that made you laugh.

1. Use the pictures below to retell the story.
Retell

2. Would Sam make a good pet? Why do you think that? Character

3. Look at page 18. Read the words. How did you know what *nab* means? Fix Up

 Look Back and Write Look back at page 17. Sam ran away. Write about why you think Sam ran.

Susan Stevens Crummel

Susan Stevens Crummel loves all animals. Her cat, Tweeter, likes to sit in the chair by the computer.

Ms. Crummel wrote poems and songs when she was a child. She even wrote skits for her sister Janet to act out for friends.

Read other books by Ms. Crummel.

Sing to the tune of "Frère Jacques."

Puppy Games

by Linda Lott

illustrated by Maribel Suarez

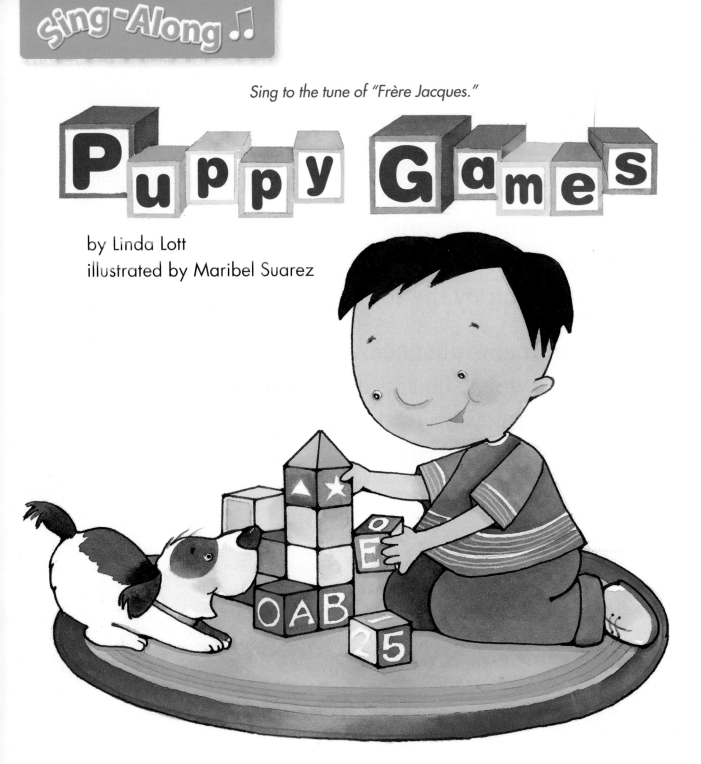

Yap! Come play now!
Yap! Come play now!
Let's have fun.
Let's have fun.

I can tug on your socks.
I'll knock over your blocks.
Then I'll nap
In your lap.

Sentences

Prompt

In *Sam, Come Back!*, a pet cat sits, runs, and hides. Think about a pet you know. Now write sentences about a pet and how you feel about the pet.

Writing Trait

Voice is the you in your sentences. It shows how you feel.

Student Model

Writer names kind of pet.

Rex is my dog.

Writer tells something pet can do.

He can play.

I love Rex.

Voice shows how writer feels about pet.

Writer's Checklist

☑ Do all my sentences tell about a pet?

☑ Do I show how I feel about the pet?

☑ Does each sentence begin with a capital letter?

☑ Does each sentence end with a period?

Grammar

Sentences

A **sentence** is a group of words that tells a complete idea. It begins with a capital letter. Many sentences end with a **period (.).**

This is a sentence. **Sam ran.**

This is not a sentence. **Al and Sam.**

· ·

Look at the sentences about a pet. Name the capital letters at the beginning. Point to the periods at the end.

Let's Talk About
Animal Friends

Words to Read

up
and
take

Read the Words

1. Pig will mix it up.

2. Pig is sad, and she is sick.

3. She will take a sip.

Genre: Fantasy

A fantasy is a story that could not really happen. In the next story you will read about a pig that does things that a real pig can not do.

Pig in a Wig

by Susan Stevens Crummel

illustrated by Janet Stevens

What will happen to this pig in a wig?

Pig in a wig is big, you see.

Tick, tick, tick.
It is three.

Pig can mix.
Mix it up.

Pig can dip.
Dip it up.

Pig can lick.
Lick it up.

It is six. Tick, tick, tick.
Pig is sad. She is sick.

Fix that pig.
Take a sip.

Fix that pig.
Quick, quick, quick!

Max, Max! Take the sax!
Play it, Max, and play it, Pam!

Pig in a wig did a jig.
What a ham!

Think and Share

Talk About It The author wrote about a silly pig. Find and read one part of the story that you think is silly.

1. Use the pictures below to retell the story.
Retell

2. Could this story really happen? Why do you think that? Realism/Fantasy

3. What are the most important things that happen in this story? Summarize

Look Back and Write Pig gets sick. Look back at pages 43–44. What makes Pig feel better? Make a list.

Janet Stevens

Janet Stevens always wanted to draw pictures. She enjoys drawing pictures for children's books.

Ms. Stevens practices drawing all the time. "Practice helps a lot in whatever you try to do," she says. She likes to draw pigs, cats, and bears.

Read more books by Ms. Stevens.

We Are Vets

by Linda Lott

illustrated by Lindsey Gardiner

Sing to the tune of "Three Blind Mice."

We are vets.
We are vets.
We help pets.
We help pets.

48

If you have a dog who is feeling sick,
Bring him to me, and I'll fix him quick.
His tail will wag, and he'll chase a stick.
He'll feel fine.
He'll feel fine.

Captions

Prompt

In *Pig in a Wig,* pictures help tell the story of a funny pig. Think about what each picture shows.

Now write two sentence captions about two of the pictures.

Writing Trait

Conventions are rules that make writing clear.

Student Model

Each caption tells about a picture.

Each caption tells a complete idea.

Writer follows <u>conventions</u> for writing sentences.

Caption for picture on page 36

A red wig is on Pig.

Caption for picture on page 44

Max plays the sax.

Writer's Checklist

☑ Does each caption tell about a picture in the story?

☑ Is each caption a complete sentence?

☑ Can readers tell whom or what sentences are about?

☑ Does each sentence begin with a capital letter and end with a period?

Grammar

Naming Parts of Sentences

A sentence has a **naming part.** It names a person, place, animal, or thing. The naming part tells whom or what the sentence is about.

Whom is this sentence about?

The pig did a jig.

The pig is the naming part of this sentence.

· ·

Look at the captions. Write the naming part of each sentence.

Let's Talk About
Animal Friends

Words to Read

help
get
use

54

Read the Words

1. Ox can help.

2. He will get a mop from Mom and Pop.

3. He will use big pans.

The Big Blue Ox

Genre: Animal Fantasy
An animal fantasy is a make-believe story with animals that act like people. Next you will read about an ox that acts like a person.

The Big Blue Ox

by Susan Stevens Crummel

illustrated by Janet Stevens

**How can this
big blue ox help?**

57

Mom and Pop have a big blue ox.

Ox can help. He is big.
He can pick, and he can dig.

Pigs in wigs sit in mud.
Ox can help!

Get the mop from Mom and Pop.
Mop the pigs. Fix the wigs.

Off to town go Mom and Pop.
Ox can help! Hop on top.

Get the cans. Pack the sack.
Ox can help! Take it back.

Ox can help! Use big pans.
He is hot. Use big fans!

Mom and Pop nap on Ox.
Ox is a big, big help.

Think and Share

Talk About It How is Ox helpful? Find and read one part of the story that shows how helpful he is.

1. Use the pictures below to retell the story.
Retell

2. Where does this story take place? What other stories does it remind you of? Setting

3. What pictures did you see in your mind of Ox helping? Visualize

 Look Back and Write Look back at the story. Write some things Ox can do to help.

Susan Stevens Crummel and Janet Stevens

Susan Crummel and Janet Stevens are sisters! They have fun working together. Ms. Crummel writes down ideas and turns them into a story. She sends the story to her sister Janet, who draws pictures to fit the story.

Read other books by Ms. Crummel and Ms. Stevens.

They Can Help

by Pat Waris

We can use help.
Can we get help?

The big dog can help.

The little dog can help.

The big dog can help.

The little dog can help.

In what ways
do they help?

Write Now

Writing and Grammar

Sentences

Prompt

In *The Big Blue Ox,* an animal helps two people.
Think about how animals help people.
Now write sentences that tell what animals do to help people.

Writing Trait

Sentences tell complete ideas.

Writer tells about two animals.

Writer tells how animals help people.

Student Model

Dogs play with us.

Cows give us milk.

Sentences begin with capital letters.

72

Writer's Checklist

☑ Do all my sentences tell about animals helping people?

☑ Does each sentence tell a complete idea?

☑ Do clear words tell what the animals do?

☑ Does each sentence end with a period?

Grammar

Action Parts of Sentences

A sentence has an **action part.** It tells what a person or thing does.

Ox helps Mom and Pop.

Naming Part	Action Part
Ox	helps Mom and Pop

. . . .

Look at the sentences about animals helping people. Write the action part in each sentence.

Let's Talk About
Wild Animals

Words to Read

this
her
too
eat

Read the Words

1. This fox naps on the rocks.

2. Her little kit sits up.

3. The fox sits up too.

4. The fox and kit will eat.

Genre: Nonfiction
Nonfiction tells facts about the real world. Next you will read about a fox and her kit at the zoo.

A Fox and a Kit

by Leya Roberts

illustrated by Charles Santore

RED FOX

How does a mother fox
take care of her kit?

This fox naps on the rocks.
Her kit naps on the rocks too.

The kit sits up.
His mom sits up.

This man is fixing dinner.
The kit will eat.
His mom will eat.

The kit is licking his lips.
His mom is licking her lips.

The kit is playing.

His mom is playing.

The kit nips and tags his mom.

The kit plays on the rocks.
His mom will get him.
She picks him up and takes him back.

The fox will watch her kit.
The kit will watch his mom.

We like watching this kit
and his mom too!
We can watch lots of animals.

Think and Share

Talk About It The author wrote *A Fox and a Kit* to tell us about foxes. Find and read one thing you learned about foxes.

1. Use the pictures below to summarize what you read. Retell

2. What is this selection mostly about? Main Idea

3. What questions about foxes did you have as you read this selection? Ask Questions

Look Back and Write Look back at page 85. Write about how the fox picks up her kit.

Meet the Illustrator
Charles Santore

Charles Santore went to a zoo to learn about foxes. Mr. Santore also put pictures of foxes all around his studio to help him paint the pictures he needed for this story. Animals are a big part of his work.

Read more books by Charles Santore.

The Zoo in the Park

Sing to the tune of "Here We Go Round the Mulberry Bush."

Here we go to the zoo in the park,

The zoo in the park, the zoo in the park.

Here we go to the zoo in the park,

So early in the morning.

illustrated by Jui Ishida

This is the way the kangaroo hops,
The kangaroo hops, the kangaroo hops.
This is the way the kangaroo hops,
So early in the morning.

This is the way the monkey jumps,
The monkey jumps, the monkey jumps.
This is the way the monkey jumps,
So early in the morning.

Titles

Prompt

The title of *A Fox and a Kit* tells what the selection is about. Think about what each page of the selection is about. Now write titles for two of the pages.

Writing Trait

Choose words that make your titles clear.

Student Model

Each title tells what the page is about.

Most words in the titles begin with capital letters.

Writer <u>chooses</u> clear <u>words.</u>

Title for page 80

Fox and Kit on the Rocks

Title for page 82

Dinner for Fox and Kit

Writer's Checklist

✓ Does each title tell what the page is about?

✓ Are words in each title in the right order?

✓ Do the words make the titles clear and interesting?

✓ Do some words in the titles begin with capital letters?

Grammar

Word Order

The **order** of words in a sentence must make sense.

These words are not in the right order.

The eat will kit.

Now the words are in the right order.

The kit will eat.

· ·

Check the order of the words in each title.
Do the words make sense in this order?

Let's Talk About
Wild Animals

Words to Read

saw

tree

your

small

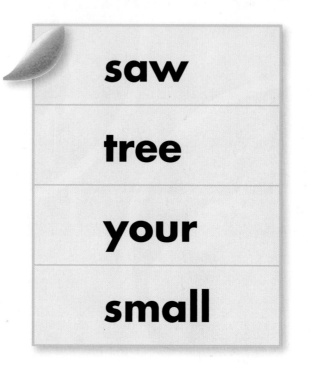

Read the Words

1. Kim saw Brad.

2. Brad was at the tree.

3. I see eggs in your tree, Brad.

4. Kim and Brad saw six small eggs in the tree.

Genre: Realistic Fiction
Realistic fiction is a made-up story that could happen. In the next story you will read about a boy and a girl like you.

Get the Egg!

by Alyssa Satin Capucilli

illustrated by Bernard Adnet

**Can Brad and Kim help
save the red bird's egg?**

Kim saw Brad at the tree.
A big red bird is in its nest, Kim.

Yes, Brad.
Six small eggs are in the nest too.

Snap! A big twig hit the nest!
Snap, snap!
The big twig hit an egg!

Stop the egg, Brad. Stop it!
Can you get the egg?

The net! Get your net, Brad.
You can help.
Get the egg in your net.

Yes! You did it, Brad.
You can help too, Kim.
Set the egg back in the nest.

Kim saw Brad at the tree.
The big red bird is back, Kim.

Yes, Brad.
The big red bird is in its nest.
Six small birds are in the nest too!

Think and Share

Talk About It This story is about a boy and a girl like you. Find and read one part of the story that you think is exciting.

1. Use the pictures below to retell the story. **Retell**

2. Could this story really happen? Why or why not? **Realism/Fantasy**

3. Does the story have a happy ending? Explain. **Story Structure**

Look Back and Write Look back at page 102. Write about what happened to the egg.

Alyssa Satin Capucilli

Alyssa Satin Capucilli writes stories in a notebook she calls her "treasure keeper." Ms. Capucilli once saved a bird that had fallen from its nest. She wrote *Get the Egg!* when she remembered how proud she felt after saving the bird.

Read other books by Alyssa Satin Capucilli.

Help the Birds

Birds like to eat. You can help.

1 Get a small twig.

2 Dip it here.

3 Dip it in this.

4 Clip it to your tree.
Watch the birds come.

Birds I Saw

Write Now

Writing and Grammar

Answers

Prompt

In *Get the Egg!,* two children help a bird that lives in a tree. Think about a wild animal that lives in a yard or a park. Now write answers to these questions: *What is the animal? What does the animal do?*

Writing Trait

Put your ideas in the right **order.**

Student Model

Writer answers first question.

The animal is a bee.

It finds flowers.

Writer answers second question.

It makes honey.

Order of ideas makes sense.

112

Writer's Checklist

✓ Do all my sentences answer the two questions?

✓ Are my ideas in an order that makes sense?

✓ Do sentences have a naming part and an action part?

✓ Does each sentence begin with a capital letter and end with a period?

Grammar

Telling Sentences

A **telling sentence** tells something. It is a statement. It begins with a **capital letter.** It ends with a **period (.).**

Kim saw Brad at the tree**.**

· ·

Look at the answers to the questions. How do you know that the answers are telling sentences?

Let's Talk About
Wild Animals

Words to Read

home

many

them

into

Read the Words

1. This is home to many big animals.

2. Will we see them?

3. We see big animals stomp into the pond.

Animal Park

Genre: Photo Essay
A photo essay uses photos and words to explain about the real world. Next you will read about some interesting wild animals.

Africa

Animal Park

by Judy Nayer

What will we see
in the big park?

The sun is up at camp.
Camp is in a big, big park.

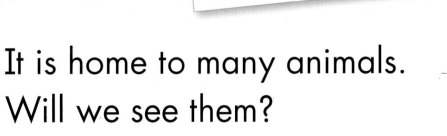

It is home to many animals.
Will we see them?

We go bump, bump, bump
in the truck.
A band of zebras runs past.
They blend into the grass.

Big cats rest from a hunt.
Cubs bat at bugs.

Big birds stand in the grass.
They can run fast!

Big hippos sit in mud.
The sun is hot, but the mud is not!

Are we in luck? Yes!
Big elephants stand and sip
in the pond.
They stomp into the pond and swim.

Bump, bump, bump!
We are back at camp.

This park is home to many animals.
We are glad we saw them!

Think and Share

Talk About It Put yourself in the animal park. Read the part of the selection that tells about the animals you would like to see.

1. Use the pictures below to tell what you learned about wild animals. Retell

2. Why do hippos sit in the mud? Cause/Effect

3. Look back at page 122. How did the pictures help you understand the words? Monitor/Fix Up

Look Back and Write Choose a photo from the selection. Write about the animal.

Meet the Author

Judy Nayer

Maybe you have seen big animals in a zoo. Judy Nayer wanted to show you where some of these animals really live, in Africa. Ms. Nayer writes every day. She says, "I often work late at night, when it's very quiet."

Read more books by Judy Nayer.

Read Together

My Dog Rags

I have a dog and his name is Rags.
He eats so much that his tummy sags.
His ears flip-flop and his tail wig-wags,
And when he walks he zig-zig-zags!

Raccoon *by Betsy Lewin*

Raccoons are not a fussy clan
when it comes time to eat.

They'll even raid a garbage can
to find a midnight treat.

130

The Hippo
by Douglas Florian

By day the hippo loves to float
On swamps and lakes, much like a boat.
At night from water it retreats,
And eats

    and eats

       and eats

         and eats.

*illustrated by
Patrice Aggs*

131

Sentences

Prompt

In *Animal Park,* visitors see wild animals, such as lions. Think about this question: *Why do lions rest after a hunt?* Now write the question. Write sentences that tell why.

Writing Trait

Sentences should **focus** on answering the question.

Student Model

Each sentence <u>focuses</u> on one <u>idea</u>.

Two good reasons answer question.

Exact words make ideas clear.

Why do lions rest after a hunt?

• They get tired when they hunt.

• They are full after they hunt.

132

Writer's Checklist

☑ Do my sentences answer the *why* question?

☑ Are words in my sentences in the right order?

☑ Do I end the question with a question mark?

☑ Do I end each statement with a period?

Grammar

Questions

A **question** is an asking sentence.

It begins with a **capital letter.**

It ends with a **question mark (?).**

Will we see the animals**?**

Are the hippos in the mud**?**

. . . .

Look at the model. How do you know which sentence is a question and which sentences are statements?

Wrap-Up

Read Together

Kitten or Lion

connect to
SCIENCE

In Unit 1, you have read a lot about animals, both pets and wild animals. How are pets and wild animals alike? How are they different?

Pets   Wild

Both

How are people and animals important to one another?

Animal Homes

connect to SCIENCE

People live in houses. In *Animal Park*, animals live and run in the wild. Write about your favorite animal and where it might live. Draw a picture to show it.

Great Helpers

connect to SOCIAL STUDIES

In *The Big Blue Ox* and *Get the Egg!*, animals help people and people help animals. Think of other ways people and animals can help one another. Share ideas with a partner.

Pictionary

Pets

puppy

dog

gerbil

kitten

cat

guinea pig

turtle

hamster

parakeet

goldfish

Pictionary

Farm Animals

chick

hen

rooster

horse

sheep

goat

pony

pig

ox

cow

calf

137

Pictionary

Wild Animals

chipmunk

squirrel

kangaroo

raccoon

skunk

snake

mole

elephant

fox

giraffe

gorilla

panda bear

bear

deer

hippopotamus

camel

tiger

lion

zebra

Pictionary

Birds

woodpecker

hummingbird

goose

robin

crow

eagle

cardinal

duck

owl

penguin

pigeon

seagull

Pictionary

Insects and Bugs

ant

caterpillar

butterfly

ladybug

bee

fly

lightning bug

beetle

spider

grasshopper

cricket

141

Pictionary
Water Animals

frog

lobster

octopus

fish

seal

polar bear

shark

alligator

dolphin

manatee

whale

Tested Words

Sam, Come Back!

in
on
way

Pig in a Wig

and
take
up

The Big Blue Ox

get
help
use

A Fox and a Kit

eat
her
this
too

Get the Egg!

saw
small
tree
your

Animal Park

home
into
many
them

Acknowledgments

Text

Page 130: "Raccoon" from *Animal Snackers* by Betsy Lewin, Henry Holt and Company, LLC, 2004. Reprinted by arrangement with the author.

Page 131: "The Hippo" from *Mammalabilia,* copyright © 2000 by Douglas Florian, reprinted by permission of Harcourt, Inc.

Illustrations

Cover: Daniel Moreton

8, 134-135 Mark Buehner

11-23, 28-47, 143 Janet Stevens

26-27 Maribel Suarez

48-49 Lindsey Gardiner

74 Hector Borlasca

75-87, 92-93 Charles Santore

90 Jui Ishida

94-113 Bernard Adnet

130-131 Patrice Aggs

Photographs

Every effort has been made to secure permission and provide appropriate credit for photographic material. The publisher deeply regrets any omission and pledges to correct errors called to its attention in subsequent editions.

Unless otherwise acknowledged, all photographs are the property of Scott Foresman, a division of Pearson Education.

Photo locators denoted as follows: Top (T), Center (C), Bottom (B), Left (L), Right (R), Background (Bkgd).

10 ©Frank Siteman/Stock Boston

11 ©Royalty-Free/Corbis

30 Tracy Morgan/©DK Images

31 (TL) ©Kaz Chiba/Getty Images, (TR) ©LWA- JDC/Corbis, (BL) ©The York Dispatch-Jason Plotkin/AP/Wide World Photos

52 ©Alan Oddie/PhotoEdit

53 (T) ©Royalty-Free/Corbis, (C) ©Steve Thornton/Corbis, (BL) ©Royalty-Free/Corbis

68 Getty Images

69 ©Mark Richards/PhotoEdit

70 ©Peter Olive/Photofusion Picture Library/Alamy Images

71 (TL) ©Bryan & Cherry Alexander Photography, (TR) ©A. Ramey/PhotoEdit, (C) ©Dallas and John Heaton/Corbis

74 (CL) ©Gallo Images/Corbis, (BC) ©Handout/Reuters/Corbis

75 (TR) ©Karl Ammann/Corbis, (CL) ©Peter Weimann/Animals Animals/Earth Scenes

89 (TR) Charles Santore/Photo ©Marianne Barcellona, (CL) Charles Santore

94 (TL) ©Niall Benvie/Corbis, (BR) ©Jean Paul Ferrero/Ardea

95 (CL) ©Dennis Avon/Ardea, (TR) ©John Mason (JLMO)/Ardea

114 ©Ron Sachs/Sygma/Corbis

115 (BR) ©Peter Johnson/Corbis, (TL) ©David Muench/Corbis, (TR) ©Michael & Patricia Fogden/Corbis, (BL) ©Tim Davis/Corbis

116 Digital Vision

118 (TL) Getty Images, (Bkgd) ©Tim Davis/Corbis

120 (Bkgd) Photo Researchers, Inc., (BR) ©Craig Lovell/Corbis

121 (L) ©Staffan Widstrand/Corbis, (TR) Digital Stock, (CR) Digital Vision, (BR) Getty Images, (Bkgd) ©Tom Nebbia/Corbis

122 (T) Brand X Pictures, (Bkgd) Tom Nebbia/Corbis

123 (TC) ©Tom Brakefield/Corbis, (CC) ©Art Wolfe Inc.

124 (TC) ©Beverly Joubert/NGS Image Collection, (BC) ©Peter Johnson/Corbis

125 ©Michele Burgess/Index Stock Imagery

126 ©Theo Allofs/Stone/Getty Images

127 (TL) Brand X Pictures, (CL) ©Norbert Rosing/NGS Image Collection, (BL) ©David Young-Wolff/Alamy Images, (Bkgd) Digital Vision

129 Digital Stock

132 ©Michele Burgess/Index Stock Imagery

133 ©Staffan Widstrand/Corbis

135 (BR) ©Dennis MacDonald/PhotoEdit, (BC) ©David Young-Wolff/PhotoEdit

136 (BCL) Karl Shone/©DK Images, (TR) Jane Burton/©DK Images, (CC) ©Richard Kolar/Animals Animals/Earth Scenes, (CL) Marc Henrie/©DK Images, (BL) Getty Images, (CR, BR) Paul Bricknell/©DK Images, (TL) ©DK Images

137 (CL) Dave King/©DK Images, (BCC) Bob Langrish/©DK Images, (BCR) ©DK Images, (TC) Mike Dunning/©DK Images, (TL) Jane Burton/©DK Images, (BC, BR, TR, TCC) Gordon Clayton/©DK Images, (TCR) Dave King/©DK Images, (BL) ©Ike Geib/Grant Heilman Photography

138 (BR) ©DK Images, (TR) Geoff Dann/©DK Images/Getty Images, (CR) Frank Greenaway/©DK Images/Getty Images, (CC) ©Dr. Harvey Barnett/Peter Arnold, Inc., (TL) ©Gary W. Carter/Corbis, (BL, TC) Jane Burton/©DK Images, (BCL) ©David Tipling/Getty Images, (TCL) ©W. Perry Conway/Corbis

139 (TL) ©Jim Zuckerman/Corbis, (BL) Dave King/©DK Images/Getty Images, (BC, TCC) Dave King/©DK Images, (TR) ©A. Ramey/PhotoEdit, (BCR, BR) Philip Dowell/©DK Images, (TC) Geoff Brightling/©DK Images, (BCC) ©David Madison/Bruce Coleman Inc., (TCR) ©S. J. Krasemann/Peter Arnold, Inc.

140 (TL) ©Roy Rainford/Robert Harding World Imagery, (TC) ©Ray Coleman/Photo Researchers, Inc., (TR) ©Tom McHugh/Photo Researchers, Inc., (TCR) ©Jeff Lepore/Photo Researchers, Inc., (BCL) ©Bill Dyer/Photo Researchers, Inc., (BCC, BCR) Cyril Laubscher/©DK Images, (BL) ©Galen Rowell/Corbis, (BC) ©John Edwards/Getty Images, (BR) ©Dinodia/Omni-Photo Communications, Inc., (TCL) © Arthur Morris/Corbis, (TCC) ©Darrell Gulin/Corbis

141 (TCL) Neil Fletcher/©DK Images, (BR) ©Simon D. Pollard/Photo Researchers, Inc., (BC, TCC) Frank Greenaway/©DK Images, (TL) Brand X Pictures, (TC) ©Cyndy Black/Robert Harding World Imagery, (TR) ©Rudi Von Briel/PhotoEdit, (BCL) ©DK Images, (BCR) Colin Keates/©DK Images, (BCC) ©Robert & Linda Mitchell, (BL) Getty Images

142 (TC) Colin Keates/©DK Images, (BL) ©Frank Staub/Index Stock Imagery, (TCC) ©Joe McDonald/Corbis, (BCC) ©Jim Stamates/Getty Image, (TR) Frank Greenaway/©DK Images, (TCL) Getty Images, (TL) ©DK Images, (BCL) ©Lionel Isy-Schwart/Getty Images, (BCR) Digital Stock, (TCR) ©Ralph Lee Hopkins/Wilderland Images, (BR) ©Brandon D. Cole/Corbis

144